One Big Union of All the Workers

Solidarity and the Fighting IWW

John Newsinger

About the author
John Newsinger is a long-standing member of the Socialist Workers Party. He has been a senior shop steward in the Amalgamated Union of Engineering Workers (AUEW), a school rep in the National Union of Teachers (NUT) and branch chair in the University and College Union (UCU). He is the author of numerous books including *Orwell's Politics* (Macmillan, 2000); *Fighting Back: The American Working Class in the 1930s* (Bookmarks, 2012); *The Blood Never Dried: A People's History of the British Empire* (Bookmarks, 2013); *Jim Larkin & the Great Dublin Lockout of 1913* (Bookmarks, 2014); *British Counterinsurgency* (Palgrave Macmillan, 2015); *The Revolutionary Journalism of Big Bill Haywood: On the Picket Line with the IWW* (Bookmarks, 2016) and co-author with Tim Sanders of the graphic novel *1917: Russia's Red Year* (Bookmarks, 2016).

One Big Union of All the Workers

Solidarity and the Fighting IWW

John Newsinger

Bookmarks Publications

One Big Union of All the Workers:
Solidarity and the Fighting IWW
John Newsinger

Published 2017 by Bookmarks Publications
c/o 1 Bloomsbury Street, London WC1B 3QE
© Bookmarks Publications
Cover design by Ben Windsor
Cover picture: Illustration from an early IWW publication.

Printed by Melita Press
ISBN print edition: 9781910885567
ISBN Kindle: 9781910885574
ISBN e-Pub: 9781910885581
ISBN PDF: 9781910885598

Contents

Introduction

From the time of its foundation in 1905 through to the repression of the war years that culminated in the great Chicago trial in 1918, the Industrial Workers of the World (IWW or Wobblies) fought tirelessly for a socialist revolution in the United States. The determination, ingenuity and courage of its members in the face of brutal, often murderous opponents still remains an inspiration to socialists throughout the world today.

This volume is certainly not intended as a full history of the IWW, but merely as an introduction to that history, hopefully encouraging the reader to both learn more about and to be enthused and inspired by the battles fought by this remarkable organisation. And, of course, the history of the IWW continued into the post-war years in the United States and indeed continues today. Nevertheless, part of the argument put forward here is that in the post-war period, the revolutionary politics of the IWW were superceded, not just in the United States but worldwide.

As Jim Cannon, a former Wobbly and Communist and later one of the founders of American Trotskyism, put it, the IWW was "the great anticipation". Even so there is still much that we can learn from the IWW. And their revolutionary example, mistakes and all, remains exemplary.

"Founded on the class struggle": The birth of the IWW

On Tuesday 27 June 1905, Bill Haywood of the Western Federation of Miners (WFM) called the first and founding convention of the IWW to order. He told the 200 delegates and observers assembled in Brand's Hall, Chicago, that they had come together "to confederate the workers of this country into a working class movement that shall have for its purpose the emancipation of the working class". It was their intention to give the working class "control of the machinery of production and distribution, without regard to capitalist masters". They recognised that "there is a continuous struggle between the two classes", the capitalist class and the working class, and consequently "this organisation will be formed, based and founded on the class struggle, having in view no compromise and no surrender".

The convention brought delegates from 43 organisations representing some 60,000 workers together with a number of individuals, including Lucy Parsons, the African American anarchist and widow of one of the Haymarket martyrs (four US political prisoners who were hanged in Chicago in November 1887); Mother Jones, the mineworkers' organiser; and Eugene Debs, the leader of the left wing of the reformist Socialist Party and himself a veteran trade unionist. Also attending the convention was Daniel De Leon, the autocratic leader of the Socialist Labour Party (SLP), a theoretically rigid and sectarian Marxist organisation. They gathered in response to what they saw as a crisis within the US labour movement where the conservative union leaders of the American Federation of Labour (AFL) were failing to defend the working class against the attacks of a rapacious, brutal capitalist class.

Many American employers were prepared to resist union-isation by armed force, employing their own armed guards and hiring private detective agencies to break strikes and smash union organisation. The methods that the employers used to keep out the unions extended from blacklisting all the way through to assassination. Trade unions in the United States were at best only semi-legal and often operated in police state conditions, except that unlike Tsarist Russia, the secret police were privatised, the likes of the Pinkertons, Baldwin-Felts, Thiel and the Burns Agencies and hundreds of other outfits, large and small. The Pinkertons alone had some 30,000 agents on their books. The labour spy operat-ing in the workplace and the union branch was part of the everyday experience of the trade union activist in the United States, something most history books neglect.

The AFL was completely incapable of taking on these employers. Instead of uniting the working class, it divided them, first of all by craft and then by often refusing to organ-ise black workers, women workers, immigrant workers and unskilled workers. Solidarity was opposed by the union leaders, with union members routinely crossing the picket lines of another union, even one attempting to organise in the same industry. The unions were dominated by corrupt bureaucrats who preached class collaboration, argued that the capitalists and the workers had the same interests and actively opposed militancy. These were capitalism's "labour lieutenants". Indeed, many of these men aspired to become capitalists themselves. They often never bothered to main-tain even the pretence of democracy, but ruled as autocrats, prospering while their members were ground down.

As Debs told the convention, the "pure and sim-ple unionism" championed by the AFL "has long since outgrown its usefulness". It was not only in the way of progress, but "has become positively reactionary, a thing that is but an auxiliary of the capitalist class". To all intents and purposes, the AFL "is today under the control of the capitalist class". Recent often bitterly fought strikes that had all ended in defeat proved as much. He called for the establishment of a new union movement "based on the class struggle". Another delegate, William Trautmann of the United Brewery Workers, one of the convention organisers, proclaimed their objective as to establish "revolutionary syndicalism" in the United States.

In place of the AFL, the convention determined to build a new union movement, the Industrial Workers of the World, democratic through and through and based on industrial organisation whereby all the workers in one industry would be organised in the same union. The employers would be unable to play the different crafts off against each other or divide the skilled from the unskilled, men from women, black from white, native from immigrant. Instead they would confront a united union movement founded on militancy and solidarity, on the principle that "an Injury to One is the Concern of All", organising the whole working class for the eventual takeover of the means of production and the establishment of socialism.

Lucy Parsons warned the delegates that the capitalist class will never "allow you to vote away their property". Instead, it "means a revolution" and the instrument for accomplishing this revolution was the general strike. The convention passed a resolution enthusiastically supporting the revolution that was under way in Russia, urging "our Russian fellow-workmen on in their struggle" and promising all the support and assistance they could "to our persecuted, struggling and suffering comrades in far-off Russia". Events in Russia were seen as demonstrating the efficacy of the general strike and Haywood looked forward to the day when American workers "will rise in revolt against the capitalist system as the working class in Russia is today".

The opening sentiments of the new union movement's Preamble summed up its philosophy: "The working class and the employing class have nothing in common... Between these two classes a struggle must go on until the workers of the world organise as a class, take possession of the earth and the machinery of production, and abolish the wage system". Militancy and solidarity were the watchwords. This spirit was to involve the IWW in massive struggles across the United States and see it face repression on a scale never seen before or since in that country. The Wobblies, as IWW members came to be called, were to write a heroic chapter in the history of the international working class movement.

2

"Undesirable citizens": The attempt to lynch Bill Haywood

The most important constituent of the newly formed IWW was the Western Federation of Miners (WFM). Under the leadership of Bill Haywood and Charles Moyer, the WFM fought strikes in the West that sometimes assumed the dimensions and characteristics of small wars. The mining companies brought in armed guards and private detectives to protect imported scabs and the WFM armed to defend itself. A year long strike in Colorado in 1903-1904 had seen the state governor mobilise the militia to protect the mines, with the union eventually going down to defeat in the face of the proclamation of martial law. By the end of the strike, 42 men had been killed, 1,345 interned without trial and 773 forcibly deported from the State. It was this experience that convinced the WFM that a new union movement was necessary.

No sooner had the IWW been established than a determined attempt was made to destroy the WFM altogether by hanging its leadership. On 30 December 1905, the former governor of Idaho, Frank Steunenberg, was killed by a bomb planted by Harry Orchard, a former Pinkerton agent. The case was actually handed over to the Pinkertons who set about framing Hayward and Moyer for this and other crimes. Orchard was promised his life if he implicated the WFM. This attempted judicial lynching, which had the support of businessmen and politicians up to and including President Theodore Roosevelt, provoked a massive, indeed unprecedented, campaign of solidarity. Roosevelt famously described the WFM leaders as "undesirable citizens", prompting thousands of people to wear "I am an undesirable citizen" badges.

Huge demonstrations were held across the United States. US$250,000, a huge sum in those days, was raised for their defence and it was made clear both at meetings and rallies and in the socialist press that their execution would be met with armed resistance and strikes. Writing in the socialist newspaper, *Appeal to Reason*, on 6 March 1906, Eugene Debs threatened revolution if Haywood and Moyer were killed. He warned that the governors of Idaho and Colorado would soon "follow them", that a million revolutionaries "would meet them with guns" and threatened a general strike "as a preliminary to a general uprising". This special issue of the paper sold over 3 million copies across the West.

The threat was taken seriously. The Idaho authorities asked Roosevelt for federal troops "in the event of their being unable to keep order and suppress armed resistance". And Roosevelt himself complained that the "labour men are very ugly and no one can tell how far such discontent will spread. There has been over the last six to eight years a great growth of socialist and radical spirit among workingmen". After 18 months in jail, Haywood was acquitted and charges against Moyer were dropped. A great victory had been won.

While Haywood was inside, the IWW had been wracked by factionalism and under attack from the American Federation of Labour (AFL). It had not prospered. And while Haywood moved to the left in prison, Moyer had moved to the right, embracing class collaboration as the only way to save the union.

One place where the IWW had been successful was in Goldfield, Nevada, where the WFM had established an IWW local and unionised the whole town, starting with the newsboys. As the IWW newspaper proclaimed they had organised "miners, engineers, clerks, stenographers, teamsters, dishwashers, waiters", all into One Big Union. Wages were driven up across the board and conditions improved, including the introduction of the eight-hour day. On 22 January 1906, the town shut down for two hours while a great rally was held, commemorating the "Bloody Sunday" massacre in St Petersburg the previous year, and pledging support for Haywood and Moyer. Vincent St John, one of the IWW leaders, told the crowd: "We will sweep the capitalist class out of the life of this nation". This was the IWW dream successfully realised in one town.

Inevitably the employers counterattacked with the enthusiastic assistance of the AFL, which sent organisers into Goldfield to try and break up the IWW. For the AFL leadership, a weak, broken union, even no union, was preferable to a militant union. They were assisted by the fact that the WFM leadership had moved to the right once Moyer was released from prison and was in the process of breaking with the IWW.

The employers locked out the IWW membership across the town and the WFM negotiated a separate deal for the miners, leaving the other union members to be replaced by scabs bought in by the AFL. On 5 November 1907, there was an unsuccessful attempt to assassinate Vincent St John. He was left with his right hand permanently disabled. Now the mine owners proceeded to destroy the WFM. In December 1907, Roosevelt sent federal troops in to occupy the town and the WFM membership was locked out and replaced with scabs. Goldfield had become a non-union stronghold.

3

"Ignorant foreign labour": McKees Rocks, 1909

One of the great historic defeats suffered by the US working class was the crushing of union organisation in the steel industry. The decisive moment was the Homestead strike of July 1892 when the multi-millionaire "philanthropist" Andrew Carnegie declared the plant non-union. A pitched battle between armed pickets and Pinkerton gunmen on 6 July saw the union men victorious. The company was saved from defeat, however, when the state militia, 8,000 men, was sent in to occupy the town and protect the importation of scabs. The Amalgamated Association of Iron and Steel Workers was defeated. After this setback, the union was driven out of plant after plant, seeking to survive where it could by abject class collaboration.

Exploitation in the steel mills was savage and brutal with low wages, long hours (12 hour days, seven days a week) and appalling working conditions. Accident rates were horrific. At the Pressed Steel Car Company plants in McKees Rocks, a worker was killed on average every day.

What provoked the revolt in McKees Rocks was the Pressed Steel management's introduction of a new payments system in the summer of 1909. Wages had already been cut dramatically in response to the 1907 recession, but with the promise of their restoration once business recovered. Now, however, the workers found their already low pay cut by up to another 30 per cent.

On 12 July 1909, some 40 riveters walked out in protest and were sacked. More and more men walked out in solidarity until on 14 July there were over 5,000 men on strike. These men were unorganised, non-union and overwhelmingly immigrant, speaking 16 different languages and completely without funds. They were driven by rage and desperation.

The strikers elected a strike committee dominated by skilled men, the Big Six, and organised mass picketing to keep the company closed. An attempt to bring in scabs by boat failed after an exchange of gunfire, but some 500 deputy sheriffs and state troopers were despatched to break the blockade. Attempts to evict strikers and their families from company housing provoked fierce resistance from men, women and children, and were called off.

While the Big Six was dominated by skilled workers and preached moderation and compromise, another committee, the Unknown Committee, was set up in secret to make sure the interests of the unskilled immigrant workers were looked after. It soon took over the effective running of the strike. The Unknown Committee was made up of veteran trade unionists, socialists and revolutionaries from all over Europe. It included veterans of the 1905 revolution in Russia and three IWW members. They called on the IWW to send in organisers.

On 7 August, the company once again attempted to carry out evictions and the next day began bringing in scabs. There were continual clashes that saw one striker, Steve Howat, killed on 11 August. Meanwhile, William Trautmann, the IWW general organiser, arrived. On 17 August, 8,000 people attended an IWW rally. Within a few days the IWW had recruited 3,000 members. Among the IWW organisers involved in the struggle was James Connolly.

Violence escalated until on Sunday 22 August pickets stopped a tram and ordered Harry Exler, a notorious police thug, off the vehicle. He drew a gun and was shot dead. The pickets were then attacked by state troopers and in the battle eight pickets, two scabs and a state trooper were killed. The state troopers ran wild for two days, beating men, women and children, invading and wrecking homes and carrying out mass arrests. The strike held solid. While many AFL members sympathised with the strikers, the AFL leadership condemned them as "ignorant foreign labour, aliens".

On 25 August, Eugene Debs spoke in the town in support of the strike even though his life had been threatened. Some 10,000 people heard him describe the struggle as "the greatest labour fight in all my history in the labour movement". The strike had to be won.

Three factors were to lead to victory. The Unknown Committee made clear that for every striker killed they would retaliate by killing a state trooper. This threat was put into effect on 29 August when five company guards and police thugs were shot in retaliation for the killing of another striker. They also sent incredibly brave volunteers into the plant posing as scabs who organised mass walk-outs, although "escapes" is a more appropriate term. The scabs, many recruited straight off immigrant ships with no idea what they were getting into, were being held prisoner in appalling conditions by the thugs of the Bergoff detective agency. There were credible stories that a number of them who had tried to desert had been murdered and their bodies incinerated in the plant.

The third factor was increasing support from rank and file AFL members, including unprecedented solidarity action by railwaymen and the spreading of the unrest throughout the steel industry. In many steel mills across the country, the management headed off trouble by putting up wages.

On 7 September, Pressed Steel capitulated and the following day the strikers marched back into work triumphant. The IWW had made its mark.

4

"Gurley Flynn will be the boss": Women workers and the IWW

Only 12 of the 200 delegates at the founding convention of the IWW were women, but they included the African American anarchist and veteran revolutionary, Lucy Parsons. In her speech to the convention, Parsons urged all women to read August Bebel's Marxist account of the position of women, *Woman in the Past, Present and Future*. Here Bebel pointed out that while men were slaves, the position of women was worse because "We are the slaves of the slaves. We are exploited more ruthlessly than men. Wherever wages are to be reduced, the capitalist class uses women to reduce them". The way forward was "to organise the women".

In the discussion on the level of union dues, she reminded delegates that women textile workers in Rhode Island only earned US$3.60 a week: "They are the class we want... women who get such poor pay should not be assessed as much as the men who get higher pay". And she looked forward to the time when the workers would not "strike and go out and starve, but to strike and remain in and take possession of the necessary property of production". She urged the delegates, "men and women", to embrace "the spirit that is now displayed in far-off Russia".

From the very beginning the IWW set about organising women workers, sending women organisers out into the field. The most remarkable of these was Elizabeth Gurley Flynn, who was first arrested for her political activity when she was 16. She was one of the IWW's most popular speakers and effective organisers and was to be elected onto the union's executive in 1909, still only 19 years old. During the great Lawrence strike of 1912 one of the songs the women strikers used to sing was "In the Good Old Picket Line". It had the lines:

> Then Gurley Flynn will be the boss
> Oh, Gee, won't that be fine
> The strikers will wear diamonds in the good old picket line.

Even in a union committed to organising women on equal terms with men, there were plenty of men with sexist attitudes that had to be fought. Gurley Flynn herself complained of one local where the men kept their wives away from IWW women in case they got "queer ideas". She regularly lectured on birth control (illegal in the United States at the time); indeed, she was "besieged by women for information on this subject". It opened up "another avenue of assault upon the system", but the men, she complained, seemed oblivious to this. They had to realise that the IWW "stands for a larger programme than more wages and shorter hours, and the industrial freedom we all aspire to will be the foundation upon which a different world for men and women will be reached".

Gurley Flynn supported the campaign for women's suffrage even though she also insisted (quite correctly) that the vote "will not free women". She complained that the campaign was dominated by wealthy women and that its working class supporters were "made the tails of a suffrage kite in the hands of women of the very class driving the girls to misery and shame". The answer was for women to "find their power at the point of production where they work".

Margaret Sanger, the foremost US advocate of birth control and sex education, was recruited to the IWW cause after hearing Gurley Flynn speaking to women laundry workers on strike in New York in 1911. In subsequent years, she was arrested a number of times supporting striking workers on the picket line and was involved in organising the children's holiday scheme during the Lawrence strike of 1912.

In March 1914, she began publishing her magazine, *The Woman Rebel*, but was arrested in August for advocating birth control and also for inciting "murder and assassination" in its pages.

She had praised an attempt to assassinate John D Rockerfeller after the Ludlow massacre in Colorado. State militia and company gunmen had machine-gunned and set on fire a tent colony set up by evicted miners and their families, killing 20 people, including two women and 11 children. She urged her readers to "Remember Ludlow". While awaiting trial she wrote the pamphlet *Family Limitation* before escaping abroad. The IWW distributed 100,000 copies of *Family Limitation*.

Another IWW birth control advocate was Marie Equi, a medical doctor and open lesbian who was recruited after being clubbed on a picket line in Portland, Oregon. She was a strong supporter of women's right to abortion. During the First World War, she was to be jailed for three years for her anti-war stance. At her trial, the prosecutor told the jury that she was an "unsexed woman" and that unless she was jailed the red flag "will float over the whole world".

The IWW set about organising domestic servants and achieved considerable success in Denver, where the Domestic Workers' Industrial Union, under the leadership of Jane Street, replaced the employment agencies, only providing staff at the union rate and with union conditions. At its height the union had 6,000 workers signed up. Street recommended sabotage as a useful way of bringing the domestic employer to heel. There was even a rebel song, "The Maids' Defiance":

> We've washed your dirty linen and we've cooked your daily
>   foods;
> We've eaten in your kitchens, and we've stood your ugly
>   moods.
> But now we've joined the Union and are organised to stay,
> The cooks and maids and chauffeurs in one grand array.

Learning from the Denver success, organising work was under way in other cities, Chicago, Seattle, Duluth, Cleveland and Salt Lake City. The wartime repression swept this initiative away.

The IWW organised and fought dozens of strikes involving women workers, but was also determined to involve women in support of strikes when it was men who had walked out. They organised mothers, wives, sisters and daughters to support the picket line. In Hammond, where male workers at the Standard Steel Car Company, inspired by the McKees Rocks victory, walked out in January 1910, the IWW organised a women's battalion. On 24 January, they went into action to prevent scabs getting into the plant. One reporter wrote of how, "Armed with brooms, clubs, stove pokers, rolling pins and other kitchen utensils, hundreds of women from the foreign settlement...today joined the ranks of their striking husbands as pickets and brought about the worst clash that the authorities have yet encountered". In the clash, one woman was shot and wounded by the police and 12 were arrested. The company surrendered on 1 February.

There is only space here to briefly consider one other strike, the Little Falls strike that began on 10 October 1912 with workers at the Phoenix and Gilbert Knitting mills, walking out in protest against pay cuts. Most of the strikers were immigrant women, Italians, Poles and Slovaks.

Little Falls was a non-union town and, as the police chief made clear, that was how it was going to stay. He told the press: "We have a strike on our hands and a foreign element to deal with. We have in the past kept them in subjection and we mean to continue to hold them where they belong". The picket line was regularly attacked by the police, meetings were banned and a number of IWW organisers were arrested on trumped up charges and jailed. Socialists from the neighbouring town of Schenectady gave the strike their full support on the picket line, on demonstrations and with food and money.

On 30 October, there were serious clashes on the picket line with mounted police clubbing people down. The strikers and their supporters fought back with one policeman shot in the leg and a private detective stabbed. A number of workers were beaten unconscious. The police rampaged through the town's immigrant quarter, wrecking the Slovak Hall and arresting many of the strikers. Among those arrested was Helen Schloss, a social worker who was running the union soup kitchen. The authorities attempted to have her committed to an asylum but, as she remarked after she was released, the doctor's diagnosis was that "I am a revolutionist".

Despite the inevitable efforts of the AFL to undermine the strike, it held solid under the leadership of IWW organiser Matilda Rabinowitz and on 3 January 1913 the management capitulated and reinstated the cuts.

One boost for the strikers had come when Helen Keller, the famous deaf-blind woman and disability activist, who was also an IWW sympathiser, sent a donation of US$87 to the strike fund. The accompanying letter was read out to the strikers in which she told them that their cause was "my cause. If they are denied a living wage, I am also defrauded. While they are industrial slaves, I cannot be free".

One Big Union of All the Workers

5

"Hanging is none too good for them": IWW free speech campaigns

The IWW set about organising migratory workers across the West. In this effort it encountered fierce resistance, not least in those towns where the workers congregated looking for work and fell prey to the employment agencies that controlled the labour market. These agencies, often wholly corrupt, ripped the workers off, both for their own benefit and for that of the employers. Every obstacle was put in the way of the IWW organising campaigns. Street meetings were banned, speakers were arrested and the distribution of literature prevented. The IWW responded to this challenge with open defiance, calling on members and supporters to break the law and fill the jails. When Free Speech campaigns were launched, the word went out for volunteers to travel across country, "riding the rails", with hundreds heeding the call.

In the years before US entry into the First World War, the IWW fought some 30 Free Speech campaigns, beginning in Missoula in 1909 and ending in the bloody Everett massacre of 1916. All that varied was the degree of violence and brutality the authorities were prepared to use.

In Missoula, Elizabeth Gurley Flynn, her husband Jack Jones, Frank Little and others launched a campaign of street meetings to recruit migratory workers. When the speakers were arrested, they sent out a call for reinforcements and volunteers poured into the town "by freight cars – on top, inside and below". The jail was filled and the cost of incarceration soon made the policy unpopular. Prisoners demanded to be fed and insisted on a trial, all adding to the expense for the town authorities, and sang rebel songs non-stop. Throughout the campaign, the IWW policy was one of passive resistance and by and large this remained a feature of the Free Speech battles. With public opinion rallying to the cause, the authorities capitulated.

While the Missoula campaign was coming to an end, another was starting up in Spokane. Here, on 2 November 1909, James Thompson was arrested when he mounted his soap box to speak. A succession of others followed and by the end of the day 150 people had been arrested. The IWW hall was raided and the local leadership was arrested. The cry went out for "Men to fill the jails of Spokane" and hundreds of Wobblies travelled to the town beginning a fight for Free Speech that was to last five months. There had been some violence in Missoula, but in Spokane the police began a policy of systematic brutality to try and deter protesters. Men were brutally beaten, crammed into cells so crowded they had to stand shoulder to shoulder day and night, and starved. They were hosed down with freezing water and then left in unheated cells. Many became ill and three died from the abuse. Hundreds were hospitalised, many with pneumonia. Among those arrested was Gurley Flynn. Once again, the authorities capitulated as hundreds of determined men arrived in the town. As Gurley Flynn, not someone to bear a grudge, later observed, the "unspeakable" Spokane police chief, Sullivan, was shot a few months later "sitting at his window...undoubtedly by one of the thousands he had brutally attacked".

There were Free Speech fights in Fresno, Aberdeen, Oakland, San Francisco, Denver, Detroit, Philadelphia and elsewhere; even in Alaska and Hawaii. But the most brutal fight was in San Diego. Here the arrests began on 8 February 1912 and the town began to fill up with Wobblies. The local press demanded repression with the *Tribune* proclaiming that "hanging is none too good for them" and advocating that they should be shot. Prisoners were starved and beaten with one 65-year-old Wobbly, Michael Hoey, dying from his injuries. One Wobbly prisoner, Jack Whyte, was charged with having said "To hell with the courts". This was a lie, he said, but he would certainly say it now.

Vigilantes were given free rein to brutalise the Wobblies with prisoners being handed over to them to be beaten and deported from the town at gunpoint. Wobblies trying to get to the town were taking off the freight trains and forced to "run the gauntlet", beaten by hundreds of vigilante thugs. On 22 April, Wobbly prisoners were taken out of town, stripped naked and forced to run a gauntlet made up of over a hundred men armed with clubs, whips, pistols and rifles. They were brutally beaten. The anarchist Ben Reitman was beaten, urinated on, branded and then forced to kiss the US flag. And on 4 May, police shot dead a Wobbly, Joseph Mikolasek. So extreme was the brutality that a number of San Diego policemen actually resigned in protest. Even here though, the fight was won.

Crucial was the bravery, endurance and determination of the Wobblies and their sympathisers, but much of the labour movement rallied to their cause. AFL locals defied their national leadership and donated funds and in many towns both AFL and Socialist Party members joined in the fight. In many towns where the authorities tried to interfere with IWW organising efforts, the mere threat of a Free Speech campaign forced them to back down.

The last episode was the most murderous. In the port of Everett in August 1916 a brutal Free Speech fight began. The local police chief, Donald McRae, was a former AFL union official who had been elected to office as a "progressive". He had men beaten and deported from the town. On 30 October, 41 Wobblies were arrested, taken out of town and beaten with spiked clubs. This level of brutality led to a protest meeting in the town that was attended by over 2,000 people.

The IWW decided to send reinforcements: a boatload of 200 volunteers, who arrived on 5 November. They were met with gunfire from deputies on the shore. Men who fell into the water were fired on. By the time the shooting stopped, four Wobblies were dead and one mortally wounded on board the ship, and at least another six were dead in the water; their bodies were never recovered. So eager were the deputies that they accidentally shot dead two of their own number! Seventy-four Wobblies were put on trial for the murder of the two deputies with every intention of hanging them, but the first man to stand trial, Thomas Tracy, was found not guilty on 4 May 1917 and they were all released. No deputy ever stood trial.

6

"The IWW has stood with the Negro": The IWW and black workers

One of the great weaknesses of the US labour movement was the way that many white workers fell for the race card and played into the hands of their employers, both North and South. The concern of many white workers was to keep black workers off the job rather than to build a united movement to fight the bosses and their political representatives. They stood by while black workers were oppressed, denied the vote, discriminated against and brutalised on a daily basis. The public torture and lynching of black men and women was almost an everyday affair.

The IWW took a determined stand against this "divide and rule". While many AFL unions either denied black workers membership altogether or ran segregated locals, the IWW preached class unity. The IWW's New Orleans newspaper, the *Voice of the People*, edited by Covington Hall, made the position clear: "The workers when they organise must be colour blind...we must aim for solidarity first and revolutionary action afterwards".

The IWW recognised that there was a great deal of distrust to be overcome. For many black workers, the trade union movement behaved like an enemy, trying to deny them work or keep them in the worst paid and most dangerous jobs. When white firemen on the Cincinnatti, New Orleans and Texas Railroad went on strike in protest against the hiring of black firemen, the IWW condemned their action and supported the black firemen. "We have no sympathy for the striking firemen", the IWW newspaper

Solidarity made clear. They were guilty of "unworking class conduct" and deserved to lose. "Unity", the paper explained, "regardless of race, creed or colour, is the only way out".

The Wobblies distributed thousands of leaflets and pamphlets urging black workers to join. The message was clear: "There is only one labour organisation in the United States that admits the coloured worker on a footing of absolute equality with the white – the Industrial Workers of the World". This view was endorsed by Mary Ovington White, one of the founders of the National Association for the Advancement of Colored People (NAACP), when she wrote: "The IWW has stood with the Negro".

The IWW condemned lynching. It published a pamphlet, *Justice for the Negro*, pointing out that "two lynchings a week" was the rate at which black men and women had been killed "for the past thirty years...put to death with every kind of torture that human fiends can invent". It graphically detailed the scale of the oppression and discrimination that black workers suffered. And it went on to proclaim that the IWW was not "a white man's union, not a black man's union...but a working man's union. All the working class in one big union".

IWW members were involved in establishing the Brotherhood of Timber Workers (BTW), organising black and white lumber workers in Texas, Louisiana and Arkansas. In the summer of 1911, the employers attempted to crush the union in a general lockout that closed 350 mills. The employers admitted defeat in February 1912.

By May 1912, the BTW had some 25,000 members, half black workers and half white. The union applied to join the IWW and Bill Haywood was sent to make the arrangements. He found the workers meeting in segregated halls as they had to under Louisiana law. "This", Haywood told them, "is one time when the law should be broken".

One Big Union of All the Workers

Covington Hall supported him: "If any arrests are made, all of us will go to jail, white and coloured together". The affiliation went ahead.

The employers went on the attack with another general lockout that began that same May. On 7 July at Grabow, company gunmen opened fire on a union demonstration. Three union men and one company guard were killed, but the union leader Arthur Emerson and 64 rank and file members were arrested and brought to trial for murder. They were inevitably held in the most appalling conditions for four months but were finally acquitted on 2 November 1913. Nevertheless, the union had suffered a serious blow.

Only a few days later, on 11 November 1913, 1,300 workers walked out of the American Lumber Company's mills in Merryville, Louisiana, in protest against the sacking of 15 men. All the victimised men were white, in a clear attempt to split the workers, but the black workers joined the walkout. Scabs were brought in, but they were often persuaded to join the strike. The company decided to break the strike with brute force. Over four days, vigilante gunmen seized strikers, inflicted terrible beatings and deported them from the town under penalty of death. The strike continued for another four months before going down to defeat. By now the BTW had been smashed right across the South.

There were also important successes. The IWW was successful at building a powerful union on the docks in Philadelphia, uniting black and white dockers. Nearly half the dockers in the city were black with most of the remaining workforce either immigrants or the sons of immigrants. Leadership positions within the union were shared out equally between black and white workers.

The IWW led a militant strike in 1913 that saw fierce clashes on a picket line that was regularly attacked by mounted police and company thugs. John McKelvey, the IWW organiser, was beaten unconscious and thrown into jail, where he was held for two months without trial. Nevertheless, the union stood firm, the men united and on 28 May they triumphed, winning a wage increase, but also forcing the employers to introduce overtime rates, time and a half for workdays and double time for Sundays and holidays.

The IWW also succeeded in organising the seamen working the barges, teamsters working the docks and dockside sugar refinery and processing workers. Indeed an AFL union affiliated official complained that the IWW Philadelphia was under the "absolute control of the IWW". This was an exaggeration, but showed the fear the IWW inspired, not least because of the support it gave to all workers in struggle throughout the city.

There were further strikes on the docks in 1914, 1915 and 1916 that gave the IWW effective control of the docks. Wages were driven up from US$1.25 a day to US$4, the wages of unity.

One stand the Philadelphia dockers took that marked them out from the rest of the IWW was a decision to support the war effort. They voted not to take strike action while the fighting continued. This did not, of course, save them from repression. The cross country raids of 5 September 1917 saw six Philadelphia Wobblies arrested. The great Chicago trial in 1918 saw three of them get 20 years in prison and three of them, including the only black Wobbly in the dock, Ben Fletcher, get ten years.

7

The IWW and the Mexican Revolution

One cause that many IWW members held as dear as their own struggles in the United States was the struggle of Mexican workers, often against US-owned companies, across the border.

This concern dated back to the strike of Mexican copper miners working for a US company, the Cananea Consolidated Copper Company, in Cananea, Sonora, in June 1906. The Mexican strikers demanded the same pay as the US miners employed by the company, an end to abusive behaviour from American foremen and more generally equal treatment in their own country.

A demonstration was fired on by company gunmen, provoking a riot. In order to protect US property, nearly 300 armed men, led by the Arizona Rangers, crossed over the border from the United States to occupy the town, shooting a number of strikers and arresting others. They handed over to Mexican police and troops, who finished off the crushing of the strike movement. What particularly concerned American mining companies was the help, funds, propaganda materials and organisers given to the Cananea strikers by the Western Federation of Miners (WFM).

The US armed intervention in the strike caused outrage across much of Mexico, graphically demonstrating the extent to which the wholly corrupt and brutal Porfirio Díaz regime was a creature of US banking, railway, oil and mining interests. It helped begin the process that eventually led to Díaz's overthrow.

Fighting against the Díaz regime was the anarchist

Ricardo Magón, who had fled Mexico in fear of his life in 1904, taking refuge in the United States. Magón was the leader of the revolutionary Partido Liberal de México (PLM) and edited its newspaper, *La Regeneración*. The paper was to reach a weekly sale of 25,000. The PLM, despite calling itself "Liberal", in fact advocated worldwide working class socialist revolution, starting with the liberation of Mexico and the ending of the country's colonial relationship with the United States. For the PLM, the political stage, in its own words, was "the whole surface of the planet" and their objective was "to smash, tyranny, capitalism and authority". It had enthusiastically supported the Cananea strikers and had a close relationship first with the WFM and later with the IWW.

The PLM attempted to launch an uprising against Díaz soon after the bloody suppression of the Cananea strike in September 1906, but the attempt miscarried. In August the following year, Magón, together with other PLM leaders, was arrested and eventually bought to trial for violating the US neutrality laws. He was not released from prison until August 1910. The leader of the Socialist Party left, Eugene Debs, campaigned for his release.

While Magón was in prison, his brother Enrique together with Práxedis Guerrero assumed the leadership of the PLM. It was Guerrero who originally coined the phrase "It is better to die on your feet than to live on your knees". The PLM attempted another uprising in the summer of 1908, but coordinated police raids on both sides of the border, seizing weapons and arresting activists, effectively smashed the movement for the time being.

At the end of 1909 and into the following year, the American socialist John Kenneth Turner began publishing a series of articles in the socialist newspaper the *Appeal to Reason* and in the *International Socialist Review* (ISR), that exposed the brutal realities of class rule in Mexico and the US role in sustaining it. His "The American Partners of Díaz", that appeared in the ISR, opened with the blunt statement that: "The United States is a partner in the slavery of Mexico". It went on to detail the involvement of US companies in the exploitation of the country and how the Díaz regime waged war against its own people on behalf of the United States. The articles were collected and published as a book, *Barbarous Mexico*, in January 1911. Both the articles and book had an impact far beyond the socialist left in the United States.

Díaz's position was weakening all the time, however, and in May 1910 his regime finally fell. The moderate, Francisco Madero, replaced him as president, but from the first faced opposition both from the right and from the left. Madero had no intention of interfering with the rights of private property and was condemned by the PLM for betraying the revolution. The PLM once again stepped forward to fight for a social revolution in Mexico. In December 1910, Guerrero was killed in battle, removing the movement's most effective leader.

The PLM leadership recognised that they did not have the strength to raise the standard of revolt throughout the whole of Mexico, so instead they planned to invade Baja California on the US border, and to establish a revolutionary base from which they could then advance through northern and into central Mexico. The IWW provided them with funds, weapons and volunteers. The Wobbly volunteers elected their officers and were organised along democratic lines. Among those assisting in recruitment and fundraising in Los Angeles was Joe Hill. He was soon to cross the border to join the fight.

The IWW had always recruited Mexican workers and published a number of Spanish language newspaper in different parts of the country. Its members rallied to the PLM cause. On 28 January 1911, a small armed band seized control of Mexicali in Baja California. Early the next month rebels led by a Wobbly volunteer, William Stanley, hijacked a train and steamed into the town of Algodones, taking it by surprise attack. Soon after, Tecate was taken. Stanley was to be killed in the fighting in April. Then, on 9 May, a rebel force made up mainly of Wobblies captured Tijuana. Here they made a point of expropriating the massive San Ysidro Ranch, owned by a consortium of Los Angeles businessmen. Jack Mosby, one of the leaders of the Wobbly volunteers, issued a revolutionary manifesto in Tijuana, proclaiming that "the revolution will be carried on in all the states of Mexico until the Mexican people are freed from the present military despotism and slavery, peonage abolished and the lands returned to the Mexican people, which have been stolen from them by the Mexican and foreign capitalists".

The US authorities moved to contain the revolutionary contagion, with Ricardo and Enrique Magón both being arrested on 14 June 1911. When they were finally sentenced in January 1912, protesters fought with the police outside the court. They were not released until January 1914.

Meanwhile Madero moved against the Baja California rebels, sending troops to drive them out. The rebel forces were forced to retreat back across the border, where many of them were rounded up by US troops. Mosby, a deserter from the US Marine Corps, was put on trial for desertion and sentenced to six years. He was shot dead when he tried to escape.

There was a real fear at this point that the US government intended a full-scale military intervention in Mexico to protect US business interests. In the October 1912 issue of the ISR, Bill Haywood warned that the government was looking "for a pretext to begin the bloodletting". The working class of the two countries were "to be driven to butcher one another in the interest of a handful of capitalists". He urged preparations for a general strike to stop any intervention.

IWW efforts at assisting the Mexican revolutionaries continued even after the defeat of the PLM in Baja California. In 1913, a party of Wobbly volunteers, led by Charlie Cline and Jesus Rangel, taking weapons across the Texas border was intercepted by US troops. They were captured after a fight in which two of their number were killed, one was beaten to death and a spy working for the Americans was shot. Cline, Rangel and their comrades received sentences ranging from 25 to 99 years.

The Mexican Revolution continued with the PLM increasingly left on the sidelines. Although Magón was regarded as a popular hero in Mexico and his ideas were certainly influential, the PLM itself remained weak and ineffectual. Emiliano Zapata was certainly influenced by Magón and indeed offered a home to *Regeneración* in revolutionary Morelos, but the offer was refused. The PLM continued to preach revolution, but its forces were too weak for it to make any real impact.

This did not stop the Magón brothers being arrested yet again in the US and being tried under the Espionage Act in 1918. They both received sentences of 20 years. They were sent to join the Wobbly prisoners in Leavenworth. Ricardo Magón died in prison on 21 November 1922. It was generally believed at the time that he had been murdered either by guards or a fellow prisoner recruited as an assassin. According to Elizabeth Gurley Flynn, when he was finally buried in Mexico on 16 January 1923, 250,000 people followed his coffin.

8

Bread and roses

The IWW fought hundreds of strikes in the years before and during the First World War. The first sit-down strike in US history was staged at the General Electric plant in Schenectady in December 1906. After the sacking of three union men, some 3,000 workers, led by the IWW, occupied the plant for nearly three days. And there were many more often bitterly fought strikes, not least at McKees Rocks in 1909.

Without any doubt, however, the two most famous were the great strikes in Lawrence, Massachusetts, in 1912, and in Paterson, New Jersey, in 1913. The first of these class battles seemed to open the way for IWW organising in the east while the second seemed to close that door.

Lawrence was a textile town, dominated by J P Morgan's American Woollen Company. The town's 12 mills provided employment for over 30,000 men, women and children. The workers, many of them immigrants (45 different languages were spoken in the mills), worked long hours in appalling conditions for low wages in what was an extremely profitable industry.

What provoked the great strike was the implementation of a state law cutting the working hours of women and children to 54 hours a week, but without any increase in wages to compensate for the resulting loss of earnings. For workers already on the breadline, this meant literal starvation.

On 11 January 1912 nearly 2,000 workers at the Everett mill walked out in protest and the strike quickly spread. On 12 January workers at the Washington mill walked out and proceeded to march through the town, shutting down the other mills. "Better to starve fighting than to starve working" was their slogan. By the end of the 13 January there were 20,000 workers on strike, rising to 25,000 by the end of the month. The strikers turned to the IWW. The "Bread and Roses" strike, as it has become known, had begun.

Whereas in the west the IWW had often retaliated against employer and police violence with a policy of an eye for an eye, in Lawrence they adopted the tactic of passive resistance. While this did not prevent police brutality, it helped rally support for the strikers. To counter this, the employers tried to discredit the union by planting a dynamite cache, but it was successfully proven that this was the work of a city official.

On 29 January there were serious clashes between police and strikers when the strikers began stopping trams to search for imported scabs. Later that day a peaceful rally was attacked by the police and a striker, Annie LoPezza, was shot dead. The following day John Ramey, a Syrian immigrant, was bayoneted to death on the picket line.

The authorities attempted to defeat the strike by removing its leadership. They charged a striker, Joseph Caruso, with having fired the shot that killed Annie LoPezza and then arrested the two Italian IWW organisers running the strike, Joseph Ettor and Arturo Giovannitti, as well. They were charged with being accessories to murder for encouraging violence, even though they had not even been on the demonstration but were speaking at meetings elsewhere. And on top of that, the private detectives who gave perjured evidence of their encouraging violence were shown not to speak Italian!

The authorities intended carrying out a judicial lynching. The IWW launched a nationwide campaign to ensure the three men were not killed, with demonstrations and meetings throughout the country raising a defence fund of us$60,000.

Bill Haywood and Elizabeth Gurley Flynn arrived in Lawrence to take over the strike leadership. The strike held solid, with an attempt at disruption by John Golden of the American Federation of Labour (AFL) being successfully beaten off. He denounced the IWW as "an outlaw organisation" and condemned the strike as "a revolution". Indeed, many rank and file AFL members increasingly rallied in support of the strikers.

The streets of Lawrence were filled with troops and the courts handed down savage sentences. On one day alone, 34 pickets were each jailed for a year. Outside the Arlington mill on 21 February, thousands of women fought with police and state militia to keep out scabs.

The IWW organised a children's holiday scheme, sending the strikers' children out of town to stay with the families of union and Socialist Party sympathisers. Margaret Sanger was one of the organisers of this holiday scheme. The police intervened to prevent this, publicly beating both women and children. The children were thrown into trucks by the police and sent to the poor farm. Angry parents attempted to storm city hall in protest. This caused a national outcry with opinion turning decisively against the employers.

After nine weeks the strike was won. According to one account, some 250,000 workers in the New England textile mills won wage increases because of the Lawrence strike. Employers conceded the workers' demands to avoid action and where they didn't, workers, inspired by the example of the Lawrence strikers, walked out.

While the strike was won, the campaign to save Ettor and Giovannitti continued. They were finally put on trial at the end of September, with the Lawrence mills coming out in sympathy and massive demonstrations taking place. The IWW threatened to call a nationwide general strike if they were convicted. After a 58-day trial, they were acquitted. Caruso, the striker who was in the frame for the actual shooting, was also found not guilty.

The following year, the IWW was involved in a bitter silk weavers' strike in Paterson, New Jersey. Some 25,000 workers walked out at the end of February. Here the employers stood firm for over six months before the union went down to defeat. The workers were effectively starved back to work.

At the suggestion of the socialist journalist John Reed, the IWW attempted to raise relief funds by holding a great strike pageant at Madison Square Garden in New York. The event took place on 7 June, involving over 1,000 strikers. Even though 15,000 people saw the performance, it did not lead to any boost in the strike fund.

As far as Gurley Flynn was concerned, the strike could have been won if only they had had the resources to stay out a while longer, but as it was the dispute had drained the IWW treasury.

By the time the strike ended, 1,473 strikers had been arrested, hundreds had been beaten and five killed by police and armed scabs. In the aftermath thousands of workers were blacklisted. This was a tremendous blow. It was compounded by the fact that the IWW had also failed to consolidate its position after the strikes that it had won. Membership rose dramatically during the struggle but fell afterwards. This failure became the subject of considerable debate within the organisation. By the end of 1913, the IWW was in serious trouble.

9

To fan the flames of discontent

Song played a vital part in the struggles and campaigns of the IWW. On the picket line, at meetings, during the Free Speech campaigns, around campfires and in the prison cell, the Wobblies, men and women, sang their defiance.

In 1908 James Wilson reported from Spokane that the local Wobblies had been livening up their "agitational meetings" with "a few songs by some of the fellow workers". He went on: "It is really surprising how soon a crowd will form in the street to hear a song in the interest of the working class". The following year a Wobbly song card was produced which sold for 5 cents and this grew into the *Big Red Songbook*. The inspiration behind this was the IWW organiser J H Walsh, one of the leaders of the 1909 Spokane Free Speech campaign. The jail was filled with Wobbly prisoners, abused and brutalised, but still defiantly singing "The Red Flag" and other revolutionary songs.

From 1909 the *Big Red Songbook*, which the cover subtitle proclaimed was intended "To Fan the Flames of Discontent", was a permanent fixture of Wobbly campaigning and organising. One historian has described it as "their Bible". It was reprinted every year with cartoons and poems alongside the songs.

As far as the IWW was concerned the *Big Red Songbook* was not just a book of songs but a vital propagandist and educational tool. The songs taught the realities of class society, satirised the bosses and their lackeys and preached the need for solidarity and the role of the One Big Union in achieving liberation. As Joe Hill argued, a political pamphlet "no matter how good, is never read more than once, but a song is learned by heart and repeated over and over again". If you could put "a few cold, commonsense facts into a song and dress them up in a cloak of humour" you would reach more workers than with the written word.

There were many Wobbly songwriters but by far the most popular was Joe Hill. A Swedish immigrant, originally named Joel Haaglund, he had arrived in the United States in 1902, changing his name to Joseph Hillstrom, which he soon shortened to Joe Hill. He travelled the country, earning a living as a migratory worker and eventually joined the IWW in Portland, Oregon, in 1908. He was active in the IWW local in San Pedro, California, in 1910 and was part of the Wobbly volunteer contingent that fought in the Mexican Revolution. He was to be badly beaten during the 1912 San Diego Free Speech campaign. His great contribution to the struggle, however, was his songs.

His first known song was "Casey Jones—the Union Scab" which he wrote in 1911 to support strikers on the South Pacific railway. It was a tremendous success. Probably his most famous song though was "The Preacher and the Slave". One of the problems the IWW faced when organising migratory workers was the activity of religious groups such as the Salvation Army, or the "Starvation Army" as the Wobblies called it. "The Preacher and the Slave" both wittily and savagely skewered their pretensions. When you ask them how you are meant to live, they:

> will answer with voices so sweet: "You will eat, bye and bye
> In that glorious land above the sky;
> Work and pray, live on hay,
> You'll get pie in the sky when you die".

His "John Golden and the Lawrence Strike" marvellously satirised the attempt by the American Federation of Labour (AFL) to sabotage the great "Bread and Roses" strike of 1912.

The AFL official John Golden was sent to help the bosses fight off the IWW and suffered the humiliation of having thousands of workers marching through the streets singing:

> A little talk with Golden
> Makes it right, all right.
> He'll settle any strike,
> If there's a coin in sight
> Just take him up to dine
> And everything is fine
> A little talk with Golden
> Makes it right, all right.

As the song goes on,

> Golden thought the workers were just crazy fools.
> But to his great surprise the foreigners were wise
> In one big solid union they were organised.

Hill was effectively blacklisted on the West Coast and moved to Utah where the IWW was under sustained attack from both the employers and the local authorities. On 10 January 1914, there was a robbery at a grocery store in Salt Lake City in which two men were killed. Hill was arrested. In normal circumstances there would have been no chance of his being convicted such was the lack of evidence. His IWW involvement at a time when the union was engaged in bitter fights in Utah ensured that despite his innocence he was not only convicted but sentenced to death.

There was a massive campaign to save him, with meetings and protests held across the United States and abroad. There was a Joe Hill Defence Committee in London. In the United States, even the AFL protested the injustice of his sentence. He was executed by firing squad on 19 November 1915. His body was shipped to Chicago where Bill Haywood, Orrin Hilton and Jim Larkin spoke at his

One Big Union of All the Workers

funeral. Larkin proclaimed that Hill had remained "true to the line of working class emancipation", that he was "attuned to the spirit of the coming time" and that he had "voiced in rebellious phrases his belief in the working class". Over 30,000 people turned out for the funeral and among the banners there were those inscribed with Hill's own words: "Don't Mourn, Organise".

Let us end though with the words from another song, "Solidarity Forever", written by Ralph Chaplin, another popular Wobbly songwriter, who was to get a 20-year sentence at the great Chicago trial of the IWW in 1918:

> Solidarity Forever!
> For the Union makes us Strong.

10

Jim Connolly, Wobbly

The Irish socialist Jim Connolly, arrived in the United States in September 1903, with his wife and five children following a year later. He was at the time a supporter of the Socialist Labour Party (SLP), although he had fallen out with its autocratic leader, Daniel De Leon. Life was hard with low wages and periods of unemployment. They lived in often dire poverty, with Connolly and his wife often going hungry. In November 1905, he wrote back home of his wish "to escape from this cursed country".

From the very first, Connolly was involved in recruiting for the IWW where he lived in Newark. He was also actively involved in the campaign to save Bill Haywood and Charles Moyer from a judicial lynching in Idaho. He played a leading role in the Newark Workingmen's Defence Committee that was set up to fight for their lives. It was during this campaign that he first met the then 17-year-old Elizabeth Gurley Flynn, already a well-known orator, when she visited Newark to speak.

All this activity took place after long hours working at the Singer sewing machine factory, which he was trying to unionise. Eventually he left the Singer factory to become an IWW organiser in New York. He already had a reputation as an organiser and propagandist. The family moved to a tenement near where the Flynns, who became good friends, lived. In March 1907, together with Gurley Flynn, her father, Tom and others, he helped set up the Irish Socialist Federation (ISF). The following year, he became the founding editor of the ISF newspaper, the *Harp*.

Connolly's organising activities in New York were overwhelmed by the economic depression that engulfed the country in 1907. In New York there were over 180,000 men out of work. The streets were filled with the unemployed, often starving and homeless. He wrote sarcastically in the *Harp* that: "Our great American institution today is the breadline. Every night in New York, thousands of men and women stand in line in the public streets, waiting for their turn to receive a few crusts of bread". And protest was met with police violence that reminded him of Dublin. The police "were swooping upon unoffending crowds and smashing in heads", but it wasn't Dublin, "I was in New York during an Unemployed Demonstration. Those smashed heads did not belong to Irish rebel patriots but to American out-of-works".

In December 1908 he wrote in the *Harp* that in the United States, "The only Liberty we know today, outside the Liberty to go hungry, stands in New York Bay, where it has been placed, I am told, in order that immigrants from Europe may get their first and last look at it, before setting foot on American soil". He went on in the same article to describe the way industrial tyranny was exercised across America with workers beaten, imprisoned and shot down for daring to organise: "practically every industrial centre in the country, from Albany, New York to San Francisco, California; from New Orleans to Minnesota, has the same tale to tell of the spilling of workingmen's blood by the hirelings of the master class".

His organising inevitably brought him face to face with the American Federation of Labour (AFL). He described the members of the AFL unions as "lions led by asses". He came into conflict not only with AFL sell-out officials who worked hand-in-glove with the employers but with the right wing of the Socialist Party that supported the AFL. Indeed, on one occasion he was involved in supporting a strike at a teddy-bear factory where he discovered that not only was an AFL official advising the boss not to give in, but the boss himself was an influential member of the Socialist Party. He complained bitterly about a so-called socialist who fired workers for joining a union.

Connolly was actively involved in trying to organise the New York dockers, many of whom were Irish-Americans. He was appointed to head up an IWW organising drive on the docks. His increasing prominence led to slanderous sectarian attacks from Daniel De Leon and the leadership of the SLP (of which he was still a member – he called the SLP leadership the "Danites"). He was accused of being an agent of the Jesuits out to sabotage and divide the working class and even of being a labour spy. The attack backfired. Connolly's sacrifices for the class struggle were too well known and his abilities as an organiser and propagandist were too well respected for the slander to gain traction. Indeed, the episode helped bring about the removal of the SLP from the ranks of the IWW.

Connolly condemned the SLP for having become a sect, obsessed with theoretical purity whereas the IWW "palpitates with the daily and hourly pulsation of the class struggle as it manifests itself in the workplaces". It had brought "a revolution in the socialist situation in America".

The Wobbly effort to organise the New York docks came up against the harsh realities of mass unemployment. The employers were using the depression to smash existing union organisation and to impose wage cuts of 20 percent and more.

In 1909, the socialist publisher Charles Kerr published Connolly's powerful, closely argued pamphlet *Socialism Made Easy*, which combined propaganda for the socialist cause with a call for Industrial Unionism as the way forward. He insisted that "it is not the theorists who make history; it is history in its evolution that makes the theorists. And the roots of history are to be found in the workshops, fields and factories". For Connolly, the real battle was not that fought at the ballot box but was "the battle being fought out every day for the power to control industry and the gauge of the progress of that battle is not to be found in the number of voters making a cross beneath the symbol of a political party, but in the number of these workers who enrol themselves in an industrial organisation with the definite purpose of making themselves masters of the industrial equipment of society in general". This battle had a "political echo" though and the fight at the ballot box had to be fought. Nevertheless, the Socialist Party had to be subordinate to the Industrial Unions because, he insisted, it was they that "in the fullness of time will overthrow that political system, and replace it by the Industrial Republic". *Socialism Made Easy* sold over 40,000 copies in the United States.

While he still prioritised the class struggle on the shop floor, with the working class, including the IWW, on the defensive, Connolly became more involved in campaigning for the Socialist Party. This was, of course, before the party's right wing were able to effectively outlaw the IWW at the 1912 convention, by which time he had returned to Ireland.

The upturn in the class struggle began with the great McKees Rocks strike of 1909. The example of the McKees Rocks workers proved contagious. Connolly became directly involved in the strike of tin plate workers in nearby New Castle, where the editor of the local socialist newspaper had been imprisoned. In May 1910, he took over as editor, supporting the strike and advising the workers to stage a fighting retreat, the better to fight another day. This was his last fight in the United States. In July he sailed for Ireland. Without any doubt if he had stayed, the revival of the class struggle that the McKees Rocks strike had presaged would have seen him once again throw himself into activity on behalf of the IWW. Instead, he returned to Ireland and took the road that led to the 1913 Dublin Lockout and the 1916 Easter Rising.

11

The Battle for Butte

On 8 June 1917, a fire broke out at the Speculator copper mine in Butte, Montana. It was to cost the lives of 163 men, burned alive or suffocated. Sixty-eight of the bodies were too badly burned to be identified.

When the men had tried to escape from the flames, they found that the safety bulkheads had been cemented shut by the company. Bodies were piled up at the bulkheads. One miner, John Musevich, later to be a defendant at the great Chicago IWW trial, found 19 bodies piled on top of each other at one bulkhead. Another defendant at the Chicago trial, John Foss, remembered seeing three bodies with the broken bones sticking out of their fingers from where the trapped men had desperately tried claw their way through the concrete.

At this time, Butte was a non-union town ruled by the appropriately named Anaconda Mining Company. It controlled the local press, politicians and the police, dominating the whole state. Indeed, conditions in Montana generally were routinely described as approximating a modern feudalism more than any other kind of social or political system.

The mine companies operated a rigorous blacklist to keep militants out of the mines. Working conditions in the copper mines were savage with on average one miner being killed in an accident every week. It was calculated that men who worked down the mines for ten years had a one in eight chance of being killed and a one in three chance of serious injury. And all this time Anaconda was reaping tremendous profits from the war in Europe; in 1916 it was the fourth most profitable company in the United States.

Union organisation had been smashed in 1914 but there was considerable unrest and it was coming to a head by 1917. A leading role was played by Irish and Irish-American miners. Jim Larkin, the Irish socialist and union leader who had led the workers during the Dublin Lockout of 1913, had spoken in the town at the end of 1916. The meeting had led to the setting up of a radical Pearse-Connolly Club in which a number of Wobblies were actively involved and this was to provide the leadership for the revolt that the Speculator fire provoked.

The miners knew that mining safety regulations required that underground bulkheads should have steel doors precisely to avoid miners being trapped in the event of fire. At the Speculator mine the bulkheads either did not have steel doors or they had been sealed shut. Such was the power and influence of the mining companies that not only were the safety regulations not enforced, but the Speculator mine was found not to be at fault for the disaster by the Bureau of Mines.

Miners began walking out on strike in protest. The strikers established the Butte Mine Workers' Union (BMWU) and demanded union recognition, an end to the blacklist, an increase in pay, the firing of the state mines inspector and the enforcement of safety regulations, and the right of free speech and assembly. By 29 June there were 15,000 men on strike, not just miners but other workers who had walked out in sympathy. The strikers set up their own newspaper, the *Butte Bulletin*, edited by the electricians' leader, the left wing socialist Bill Dunne.

The mine companies responded by filling the town with armed private detectives, over 200 men from the Pinkerton, Thiel and Burns agencies. They offered to increase wages, but absolutely refused to recognise the union.

Even though the BMWU never actually affiliated to the

One Big Union of All the Workers

IWW, there was a large contingent of Wobblies involved in the struggle. The IWW national office sent one of their best organisers, Frank Little, a member of the union's five-man general executive, to help organise the fight. He arrived on 18 July and urged greater militancy on the strikers. The employers were determined to eliminate him. On 1 August, Little was kidnapped by armed men, dragged through the streets behind a car, tortured, shot and hanged from a bridge. His death was intended as a warning with more to follow.

A few days later an attempt was made to kidnap Bill Dunne, but he went armed and shot two of his attackers. The next day the local newspapers, controlled by Anaconda, somewhat prematurely reported his disappearance! The temper of the times was shown by the fact that at the *Butte Bulletin* the staff worked with firearms always within reach.

Little's assassination was known to be the work of company gunmen. Indeed, the *Butte Bulletin* actually named the killers: "William Oates, Herman Gilles, Peter Beaudin, a rat named Middleton...working under a chief gunman named Ryan". The strikers actually received the support of Jeanette Rankin, the first woman to be elected to Congress. She had been elected in 1916, was an opponent of the war, condemned Anaconda and called for the mines to be taken over by the federal government. She told the *Washington Post* seven days after Little's death that she knew Anaconda would try to destroy her, after all, "They own the state... They own the press", but she went on, "they probably won't assassinate me". She was denounced as a Bolshevik and witch-hunted out of office in 1918.

When Frank Little was buried in Butte, 3,000 mourners followed his coffin and thousands more lined the streets. His coffin was covered by a red banner proclaiming him "a martyr to solidarity".

Meanwhile, the newspapers conducted a campaign of lies and slander against the BMWU and the Wobblies.

They were accused of trying to stir up an Apache revolt and of being in league with Germany. Indeed, Zeppelin airships were even reported as being seen in the canyons of Montana, presumably communicating with their IWW agents.

And then on 30 August the employment office of Anaconda's Parrot mine was bombed, almost certainly the work of company spies. Hardly any damage was done but it provided a useful pretext for the occupation of the town by the state militia and the proclamation of martial law. The BMWU was confronted by severe repression. Military courts handed out draconian sentences. A union barber who refused to cut a guardsman's hair got 60 days. Most damaging though was the imprisonment of the union leadership, with the union president, Michael McDonald getting three years and the vice-president, Joe Bradley, a Wobbly, getting five years. Bradley was to die in prison.

In September, a company gunman shot dead a striker, John Carroll, with the local chief of military intelligence remarking that hopefully this would help break the strike but if not, "we'll kill some more".

At the same time as repression was being stepped up in Butte, the federal government moved against the IWW across the country with the raids of 5 September 1917 that put the union very much on the defensive. The IWW could offer little help to the BMWU.

The strike was broken over the winter and finally called off in December 1917. In February 1918, Montana passed a Sedition Act that effectively banned the IWW. This was not the end, however. In 1919-1920 there was to be another attempt to unionise the copper mines with the Wobblies playing a leading role. Once again the town was placed under military occupation and the union was defeated.

12

War and repression

By 1914 there was growing acknowledgement within the ranks of the IWW that despite the part that it had played in the class struggle in the United States, the strikes it had led and the campaigns it had organised, the union had not succeeded in becoming a mass revolutionary force. It had failed to sweep aside the American Federation of Labour (AFL) and lead the American working class to socialism. Great strikes had been followed by a failure to consolidate the union's position. The great victory in Lawrence had seen the IWW recruit 14,000 members, but within a year the membership had fallen to only 700.

In 1914, after years of struggle, the IWW had only 11,000 paid-up members across the country and was being written off. Its only activity in the east was among Italian bakers in New York and on the Philadelphia docks.

At this point, Bill Haywood was elected general secretary and launched organising drives in a number of industries with a determination to establish strong union organisation and to fix it permanently in place. As much effort was to be put into consolidating victories as was to be put into winning them.

The IWW put a tremendous effort into organising migratory agricultural workers, then moving into iron and copper mining, lumber, construction and oil.

As Ralph Chaplin put it, in a number of industries the IWW was taking control on "the job". This was in the face of often fierce employer resistance, violent repression and AFL scabbing. By September 1917 the IWW had over 100,000 paid up members. So successful was the union that a growing number of state governors demanded that the federal government take action to suppress the IWW.

The outbreak of war in Europe in 1914 provided the spectacle of socialist parties and trade unions rallying to their respective governments. The Russian Bolsheviks and a handful of others resisted the tide of jingoistic patriotism. In the United States there was massive opposition to becoming involved in the European conflict. The Democrat Woodrow Wilson secured re-election as President in 1916 on the promise of keeping the country out of the war. Once elected, in the best traditions of bourgeois politics, he promptly took the United States into the war.

Despite his ill-deserved reputation as a liberal, Wilson was in reality a racist and segregationist, an authoritarian who was determined to crush any and all domestic opposition to the war. Draconian laws, the 1917 Espionage act and the 1918 Sedition Act, effectively criminalised dissent. And these laws were reinforced by the actions of vigilantes who in many ways were a forerunner of post-war European fascism.

While the reformist Socialist Party took a strong anti-war stance, Haywood was opposed to the IWW becoming involved in anti-war campaigning. He was certainly opposed to the war himself but nevertheless argued that the war provided ideal conditions for building the IWW and that they should therefore focus on organising and not give the state an excuse for repression. Other leading Wobblies disagreed, with Frank Little, a strong opponent of the war, arguing that repression was going to come anyway. Little was to fall victim to the rising tide of repression himself when he was kidnapped, tortured and murdered, in Butte, Montana, in August 1917.

On 12 July 1917 in Bisbee, Arizona, a miners' strike was put down by the illegal rounding up and mass deportation of the strikers and their supporters from the town. Some

2,000 armed men rounded up hundreds of Wobblies and supposed sympathisers, including AFL members and shop-keepers. Some of them were savagely beaten in the process. Eventually some 1,200 men were herded into cattle trucks, 50 to a truck, and taken across the state line into New Mexico and abandoned in the desert. They were effectively interned in a US Army camp where they were deliberately kept half-starved and cold. Many of those deported had families, wives and children back in Bisbee.

Meanwhile a number of states, beginning with Idaho, passed anti-syndicalism laws effectively banning the IWW. The federal government finally took action on 5 September 1917 with coordinated raids on IWW offices in 33 cities. In Chicago alone, the authorities seized five tons of "evidence". IWW membership lists were handed over to the AFL so they could assist employers in the process of blacklisting.

Instead of going on the run, going underground, Haywood ordered those indicted to surrender and to fight the charges they faced in court. He actually seems to have believed that the Wobblies could successfully defend themselves. They had not campaigned against the war and the authorities would find no evidence that the union was being financed by the Germans. But while there had been notable courtroom victories in the past, not least Haywood's own July 1907 defeat of an attempted judicial lynching in Idaho, the war had changed everything.

The full-weight of the federal government was thrown against the IWW at a time when the country was in the grip of a jingoistic patriotic hysteria. It did not matter that the union had not opposed the war because the government had decided to destroy it because of its militancy and radi-calism. The IWW fell victim to a "Red Scare" that was to be intensified in the post-war years as a response to the Russian Revolution.

The Chicago trial saw the defendants testify to the

hardness of their lives and the brutality of bosses, police and vigilantes. One labour spy actually admitted in the dock that the arrival of the IWW always led to better pay and conditions for the workers. And the defence even bought before the court a succession of IWW members in military uniform to testify that the organisation had not campaigned against the war. When Haywood himself took the stand, he insisted that while he was personally opposed to the war, the IWW most certainly did not because it was not "an organisation matter". As he told the jury, "The fight of the IWW is on the economic field". When the IWW led strikes in wartime, it was not to damage the war effort but to improve pay and conditions at a time when the bosses were profiteering from the war.

After four months, the great Chicago trial came to an end on 17 August 1918. It took the jury one hour to find the defendants guilty on all the charges against them. IWW leaders were sentenced to punitive jail terms. Haywood and 14 others got 20 years, 33 others got ten years, another 35 got five years and 12 got one year. And these sentences were to be served in the harshest conditions. So much for Woodrow Wilson's liberalism! This was little better than lynch law.

There were other mass trials in Sacramento, Wichita and Omaha, Nebraska. The Sacramento trial of 54 Wobblies saw the police relentlessly harass the defence campaign. The secretary of the defence committee was arrested no fewer than 15 times and when Theodora Pollok, a middle class sympathiser, attempted to arrange bail for some of the prisoners, she was arrested, the bail money was confiscated and she was subjected to a sexual examination normally reserved for prostitutes. The Sacramento prisoners (five died in prison) all got from one to ten years in January 1919. This was, of course, long after the war had ended. Pollok got a US$100 fine for her impertinence. Alongside this judicial repression, IWW members were subject to a nationwide campaign of violent intimidation, ranging from beatings to lynching. All this during and after a war ostensibly fought "for democracy".

The IWW was successfully beaten down, forced onto the defensive and into retreat. The repression continued into the post-war years.

13

George Hardy, Wobbly

One of the 95 men sentenced at the end of the great Chicago IWW trial in August 1918 was the British socialist and syndicalist George Hardy. Much to his surprise he only received a one-year term of imprisonment, something he put down to the prosecution not realising how long he had been active in the organisation. He was certainly not the only British socialist active in the IWW at this time. And interestingly, while there was not a single protest at the sentences handed down from any AFL affiliate, there were protests from dozens of British labour organisations. Hardy's memoir, *Those Stormy Years*, published in 1956 is an invaluable account of the experiences of a British Wobbly.

George Hardy was born in 1884, the son of a farm labourer near Beverley, East Yorkshire. One of his earliest memories was of seeing the cavalry riding through his village on their way back from breaking a dockers' strike in Hull. He started work full-time aged 13. Work was casual, poorly paid and unorganised and he had regular periods of unemployment. In 1906, he became an "assisted" immigrant, shipping out to Canada in the hope of a better life.

In Canada, Hardy found the job situation much as it had been in Britain. He moved from one casual low paid job to another, often sacked for complaining about pay and conditions. And then in British Columbia he met a Swedish lumberjack, "the first Socialist I ever met to my knowledge". Together they travelled to Vancouver Island looking for work and his new companion, a Wobbly, introduced him to "the principles of industrial unionism and socialism" and gave him "an elementary education in Marxism". Hardy never forgot one crucial phrase that his friend repeated over and over: "We are robbed at the point of production".

In Victoria, he became active in the Teamsters' union, playing a leading role in a number of strikes and in the end helping to lead his union local out of the Teamsters and into the IWW. He was enthusiastically involved in spreading the gospel of militancy and industrial unionism. The IWW was actively involved in supporting the great Vancouver Island miners' strike of 1912-1914 when troops "fully equipped with machine guns and artillery" occupied the minefield and thousands of scabs were brought in, many from abroad. One of Hardy's proudest moments was when British miners from Durham who had emigrated to Canada to work in the mines arrived, promptly refused to scab and joined the strike. The miners were defeated, with thousands blacklisted, and the union was not to be recognised in the coalfield until 1938.

The outbreak of war in 1914 led to widespread unemployment and in 1915 Hardy returned home to Beverley, working on the docks in Hull as a casual labourer and campaigning against the war. Eventually, he signed up as a merchant seaman. By the summer of 1916, he decided to ship out to the United States and once again became active in the IWW. Early in 1917, he was elected general secretary of the IWW's Marine Workers' Industrial Union.

One of the problems the US labour movement faced was that posed by industrial spies. Hardy became suspicious of the chairman of the Marine Workers and arranged to have him followed. He led them to the offices of the Thiel Detective Agency. At the next meeting of the union executive, the man was exposed as a spy and thrown down four flights of stairs and out the door.

Hardy was heavily involved in the lumber workers' strikes of 1917, helping Tom Whitehead, the British secretary of the

Seattle IWW. And then, on 5 September 1917, all across the country IWW offices were raided, documents seized and members arrested. In Seattle, the police even confiscated Joe Hill's death mask. Among those arrested was George Hardy, shipped off to Chicago to stand trial, a 3,000 mile train journey, in chains all the way.

The prisoners refused to be broken. One way they kept their morale up and brought down that of their jailors was by singing revolutionary songs. Hardy remembered the song that was written in jail to celebrate the October Revolution in Russia:

> One day as I sat pining
> A message of cheer came to me,
> A light of revolt was shining,
> in a country far over the sea....
> All hail to the Bolsheviki!
> We will fight for our class and be free...
> An echo from Russia is sounding
> The chime of true liberty,
> It's a message of millions resounding
> To throw off your chains and be free.

After a trial lasting four months, the Wobblies were found guilty, sentenced, and transferred to Leavenworth Penitentiary, Kansas, to serve their time. When they arrived, the governor warned them not to cause any trouble. In response, they marched into the prison singing the "Internationale". They were almost immediately in conflict with the prison authorities.

Wobbly prisoners refused to do prison work on Saturdays. They were put in isolation cells where they slept on the concrete floor with one blanket and were put on a diet of bread and water. The hours they were supposed to be working, "they were chained up, with their hands over their heads to the top bars of the cell gates". After a fortnight the

One Big Union of All the Workers

governor gave in and Saturday working was ended.

After a protest against prison food, a number of Wobbly prisoners were severely beaten and sentenced to be held in the isolation cells. One of them, Bert Lorton, another British Wobbly from Birmingham, remained in isolation for over a year. As Hardy observed: "He was forever unrepentant".

Revolutionary literature was smuggled into Leavenworth. It was here that Hardy read Lenin's pamphlet *Soviets at Work* and began to turn to Bolshevism as the way forward.

He served his year inside and went on to become one of those urging the IWW to move in a Bolshevik direction. The attempt failed and Hardy eventually returned to Britain and joined the Communist Party. He was actively involved in the 1926 General Strike, "the highest point of struggle ever reached by the British working class". When the police raided the National Minority Movement headquarters, Hardy, who was in the building, escaped by sliding down a slate roof and then crawling over a plank onto the wall of the timber yard next door. He jumped down inside and found himself locked in because they were all on strike. He had to climb over the wall out of sight of the police.

Looking back, he admitted that they were ready for the TUC right to sell the strike out, but were taken by surprise by the capitulation of the left wing union leaders. Afterwards, he worked in the Red International of Labour Unions in China before returning home in 1929 and going to work for the Communist International. His son, George, was killed fighting the fascists in Spain.

14

The turn to Bolshevism

The October Revolution transformed socialist politics throughout the world. At a time when the most terrible war in human history (up until then) raged, the working class in Russia had overthrown the Tsarist regime in February 1917 and in October had itself taken power under the leadership of the Bolsheviks.

The Revolution not only provided inspiration in dark times, but also provided vital political lessons for socialists everywhere, including the United States. Many Wobblies were eager to learn these lessons. Their belief had been that the One Big Union, the IWW, would be built up until it encompassed the whole working class and was strong enough to overthrow the capitalist class by means of a great general strike. Confronted with a general strike the capitalist class was expected to surrender.

What was missing from this strategy was an understanding of the role of the capitalist state in the class struggle. What the Bolsheviks argued was that the revolutionary movement would inevitably come under attack from the capitalist state as it grew stronger and in a revolutionary situation would have to destroy the capitalist state if it was to succeed. The armed bodies of men that were the guarantors of capitalist power would have to be confronted, some won over or others physically defeated. Failure to do this would result in the triumph of reaction and the unleashing of an anti-working class terror.

The general strike was not the way to achieve this. Troops and police would be turned loose to massacre the strikers.

Instead it was necessary to destroy the capitalist state. The general strike was certainly a vital part of the struggle but in the end what was necessary was armed insurrection and the replacement of the capitalist state by workers' councils. This was one of the great lessons of the October Revolution: workers' councils would replace the capitalist state. The Soviets, as they were known in Russia, were not the creation of Marxist theorists, but of the Russian working class who invented them as the way in which the working class could exercise power. Not through reformist politicians in capitalist parliaments and congresses, but through their own directly elected representatives, subject to recall, could the working class rule.

For many Wobblies, the role of the capitalist state had been brought home forcibly by the scale of the repression that was unleashed against the American left in 1917 and that continued into the post-war period. The state that sentenced the IWW leadership to 20 years apiece on trumped-up charges, that had all but destroyed the reformist Socialist Party, would have to be smashed.

Another problem that the Wobblies had been wrestling with since 1913-1914 was the question of the uneven level of consciousness within the working class. For them the One Big Union was the instrument of working class liberation, but this belief had continually come up against the reality that for most workers the trade union movement was a way of improving pay and conditions under capitalism, not of overthrowing it. This was an important factor behind the IWW's failure to consolidate its position even when it won strikes. The union grew, often by the thousands, when struggle raged, but in the aftermath there was a failure to consolidate the advances made.

What the experience of Bolshevism offered was a way of working with the uneven consciousness of the working class, a way of strengthening the position of the most advanced workers and increasing their influence within the class until they were able to lead it to revolution. This required a revolutionary party working within the unions.

Before 1917, as far as most Wobblies were concerned, a political party was either altogether unnecessary or else played a subsidiary, primarily propagandist role in the struggle. The October Revolution showed that there was another way and this alternative had led the workers to power in Russia.

And the post-war experience of the American working class seemed to show that the IWW had become a dead-end for revolutionaries. There were massive working class struggles in the United States. In 1919, there were 3,630 strikes involving over 4 million workers. The employers and government responded with ferocious repression. One of the decisive battles, the attempt to unionise steel, led by William Z Foster, a former Wobbly and future Communist Party leader, went down to defeat, but only after 26 strikers had been killed, hundreds injured, beaten or shot and thousands arrested. In no other industrialised country was even basic union organisation resisted with such violence. A capitalist class that was prepared to shoot strikers down for trying to organise was certainly not going to surrender its wealth and power without a violent struggle, if necessary drowning the working class in blood. This was a crucial lesson.

The massive post-war strike wave largely passed the IWW by. Many Wobblies were involved in it, of course, sometimes even playing leadership roles, but they were mainly dual carders, members of both the IWW and of the union that dominated their workplace. These individuals were, of course, acknowledging the uneven consciousness of the working class in practice and many of them came to Bolshevism through the experience.

With both the example of Soviet Russia and their own

One Big Union of All the Workers

experience of the class struggle in the United States to learn from, many leading Wobblies embraced Bolshevism. One of them was Bill Haywood. He had read John Reed's *Ten Days That Shook the World* in prison. As far as he was concerned, the workers had taken power in Russia and now the task was to spread the revolution across the world. He told Ralph Chaplin that the Russian Revolution was "the greatest event in our lives. It represents all that we have been dreaming of and fighting for all our lives. It is the dawn of freedom and industrial democracy". Some 2,000 Wobblies, a fifth of the membership at the time, were to join the Communist Party in the United States.

The failure of the Revolution to spread was, of course, to see the dashing of all these hopes and dreams and the coming to power of the Stalin regime. Workers' power in Russia was to be replaced by a state capitalist tyranny over the working class that by the 1930s maintained itself in power by terror.

What of the IWW itself? The union still propagandised and fought for the One Big Union with its members often displaying considerable courage and ingenuity in the struggle. Despite this, when the great working class revolt of the 1930s came, the moment they had been waiting for, the IWW was once again bypassed. The great strikes and factory occupations were often led by men and women who had started out as Wobbly militants, by the likes of Harry Bridges and James Cannon, but by the time they came to transform the face of industrial America the day of the IWW had passed.

15

The road to Minneapolis, 1934

One of the Wobblies who embraced Bolshevism was Jim Cannon. He had joined the Socialist Party in 1908, but gravitated towards the IWW. He joined the organisation in 1912. Cannon was involved as an organiser in the 1913 rubber workers' strike in Akron. This strike, that at its height saw 20,000 workers out, was defeated by police and vigilante violence. When Bill Haywood arrived in the city to speak at a mass meeting, Cannon was one of those who escorted him from the station, providing protection against vigilante action.

As was usual at this time, the employers were assisted by the efforts of AFL officials to undermine and divide the workers. And the employers successfully infiltrated labour spies into the ranks of the local IWW leadership. Membership lists were handed over to the employers so that activists could be effectively blacklisted. The defeat of the Akron strike was as serious a blow to the IWW as was the defeat at Paterson that same year.

The following year, Cannon was involved in the dock strike in Duluth, working alongside Frank Little and Leo Laukki, a Finnish veteran of the 1905 Revolution in Russia.

At one point, Little was kidnapped and held prisoner by company gunmen. When Cannon discovered where he was being held, he sent some 20 armed union men to free him. After his rescue, and accompanied by Cannon, Little insisted on walking "for an hour or two around the docks, directly past all the places swarming with gunmen". He explained that it was necessary to show both the strikers and the company thugs that they were not intimidated, although as Cannon observes, the whole time Little had "a pistol in his pocket and his hand on it".

With the coming of war, Cannon was one of those who was critical of the IWW's failure to campaign against US involvement. He believed that at the Chicago trial the defendants should have proclaimed their defiance and opposed the war, rather than engage in a vain attempt to secure acquittal. He was more impressed by the stand taken by the left wing of the Socialist Party.

The war and the Russian Revolution led to him re-joining the Socialist Party. He was active within the Socialist Party left, arguing for a turn to Bolshevism and from here became a founding member of the Communist Labour Party in 1919. He was to be a leading figure in the US Communist movement until his expulsion for Trotskyism in October 1928. Cannon and his comrades established their own party, the Communist League of America.

When Cannon was expelled from the Communist Party it was in the process of undertaking its "Third Period" turn. This was a policy of sectarian ultra-leftism imposed from Moscow. It involved targeting the rest of the left as the main enemy to be fought with no-holds barred, not just lies and smears, but also the use of violence. Inevitably one of the principle targets of the Communist Party was the Trotskyists, whose meetings were broken up and whose newspaper sellers were beaten up. In this situation, the Trotskyists and the IWW came together to protect each other's meetings from Communist attack. Indeed, Wobblies even helped guard the Communist League's founding conference. The IWW, the Communist League and the anarchist group around the *Il Martello* (The Hammer) newspaper all shared the same office building through the 1930s and into the 1940s. They joined together for protection against the Stalinists.

The Third Period was a complete disaster for the international working class movement. In country after country, Communist Party sectarianism seriously weakened and divided the left. Most disastrously, in Germany, by dividing the strongest labour movement in the world, it played an essential part in allowing the Nazis to take power in 1933.

But while the German working class was experiencing a terrible historic defeat, in the United States the working class was beginning to recover from its post-war defeats. The 1920s had seen the employers confidently on top in the United States. While the onset of the Great Depression had wrecked the banking system and devastated whole industries, the working class seemed incapable of fighting back. With millions unemployed and people actually starving to death, it looked as if the ruling class were going to be able to overcome the crisis at the expense of the working class. This situation changed in 1934.

In Toledo, Minneapolis and San Francisco massive working class revolts, not too strong a word, decisively shifted the balance of class forces in the United States. These struggles were not led by the IWW, but by socialists, many of them former Wobblies, working within AFL unions. In Minneapolis the struggle was led by members of the Communist League working within the Teamsters union. A union that was notorious for its corrupt leadership was transformed in Minneapolis into a militant, democratic organisation under rank and file control. They organised on the job until in May 1934 they were ready to take on the employers in a historic fight.

The ferociously anti-union employers met the strike with violence. After pickets, both men and women, were brutally beaten, left with broken arms and legs, the union prepared a trap. Some 600 men, armed with clubs, were hidden in the AFL hall while another 900 waited elsewhere in case they were also needed. A small picket detachment was sent out inviting attack and when the police obliged, they found themselves overwhelmed with 30 of their number hospitalised.

The battle was resumed the following day, with hundreds of building workers going on strike and marching to the support of the Teamsters. This was the celebrated "Battle of Deputies Run", because that is what they did. Two deputies were killed in the fighting and the union was left in control of the Minneapolis city centre. The employers surrendered but this turned out to be only a truce.

Strike action was renewed in July and this time the police made free use of firearms. On 20 July, they shot 69 people, pickets and passersby, killing two union men. The state militia occupied the town, but the union held the line and a historic victory was won that helped transform the face of industrial America. Workers throughout the country took heart from the victory.

One of the lessons of the great strikes in Toledo, Minneapolis and San Francisco was that despite the courage, selfless dedication and determination of the membership of the IWW over the years, the working class revolt that was to culminate in the great sit-down strikes of 1937 passed the IWW by. There was no great rallying to the IWW. Instead, there was a rallying to the unions that affiliated to the Congress of Industrial Organisations (CIO) and this, as they say, is another story.

Further Reading

Stewart Bird et al, *Solidarity Forever: An Oral History of the Wobblies* (London 1987)

Peter Carlson, *Roughneck: The Life and Times of Big Bill Haywood* (New York 1983)

Ralph Chaplin (*Wobbly*, Chicago 1948)

Eric Thomas Chester, *The Wobblies in their Heyday* (Santa Barbara 2014)

Peter Cole, *Ben Fletcher: The Life and Times of a Black Wobbly* (Chicago 2007)

Joseph Conlin, *Bread and Roses Too*, Westport (Conn 1969)

Joseph Conlin, *Big Bill Haywood and the Radical Union Movement* (New York 1969)

Ralph Darlington, *Syndicalism and the Transition to Communism* (Aldershot 2008)

Melvyn Dubofsky, *Big Bill Haywood* (Manchester 1987)

Melvyn Dubofsky, *We Shall Be All* (Chicago 1969)

Philip Foner, *The Industrial Workers of the World 1905-1917* (New York 1973)

John Gambs, *The Decline of the IWW* (New York 1966)

Greg Hall, *Harvest Wobblies* (Corvallis 2001)

George Hardy, *Those Stormy Years* (London 1956)

Bill Haywood, *Autobiography* (New York 1969)

Joyce Kornbluh, *Rebel Voices: An IWW Anthology* (Chicago 1988)

John Newsinger, *Fighting Back: The American Working Class in the 1930s* (London 2012)

John Newsinger, *On the Picket Line with the IWW: The Revolutionary Journalism of Big Bill Haywood* (London 2016)

Bryan Palmer, *James Cannon and the Origins of the American Revolutionary Left* (Urbana 2007)

Carl Reeve and Ann Barton Reeve, *James Connolly and the United States* (New Jersey 1978)

Franklin Rosemont, *Joe Hill, the IWW and the Making of a Revolutionary Counterculture* (Chicago 2003)

Allen Ruff, *'We Called Each Other Comrade': Charles H Kerr and Company*, Radical Publishers (Urbana 1997)

Salvatore Salerno, *Red November, Black November: Culture and Community in the Industrial Workers of the World* (New York 1989)

Nigel Sellars, *Oil, Wheat and Wobblies* (Norman 1998)

Fred Thompson and Jon Bekken, *The IWW: Its First One Hundred Years* (Cincinnati 2006)